Leading
Professional Learning

*For my two children, Paisley and Caden. May you
accomplish the things you never dreamed possible. —Tom*

*For my former student Jason Futch, who,
against all odds, epitomizes lifelong learning.
You have taught me a great deal, my friend. —Jeff*

CORWIN
CONNECTED
EDUCATORS
SERIES

Empowered Schools, Empowered Students: Creating Connected and Invested Learners
By Pernille Ripp @pernilleripp

Blogging for Educators: Writing for Professional Learning
By Starr Sackstein @mssackstein

Principal Professional Development: Leading Learning in the Digital Age
By Joseph Sanfelippo @Joesanfelippofc and Tony Sinanis @TonySinanis

The Power of Branding: Telling Your School's Story
By Tony Sinanis @TonySinanis and Joseph Sanfelippo @Joesanfelippofc

The Relevant Educator: How Connectedness Empowers Learning
By Tom Whitby @tomwhitby and Steven W. Anderson @web20classroom

Leading
Professional Learning

Tools to Connect and Empower Teachers

Thomas C. Murray
Jeffrey Zoul

A SAGE Company

A SAGE Company

FOR INFORMATION:

Corwin

A SAGE Company

2455 Teller Road

Thousand Oaks, California 91320

(800) 233-9936

www.corwin.com

SAGE Publications Ltd.

1 Oliver's Yard

55 City Road

London EC1Y 1SP

United Kingdom

SAGE Publications India Pvt. Ltd.

B 1/I 1 Mohan Cooperative Industrial Area

Mathura Road, New Delhi 110 044

India

SAGE Publications Asia-Pacific Pte. Ltd.

3 Church Street

#10-04 Samsung Hub

Singapore 049483

Printed in the United States of America

A catalog record of this book is available from the Library of Congress.

ISBN 978-1-4833-7992-0

This book is printed on acid-free paper.

Executive Editor: Arnis Burvikovs

Acquisitions Editor: Ariel Price

Editorial Assistant: Andrew Olson

Production Editor: Amy Schroller

Copy Editor: Mark Bast

Typesetter: C&M Digitals (P) Ltd.

Proofreader: Laura Webb

Cover and Interior Design: Janet Kiesel

Marketing Manager: Lisa Lysne

SUSTAINABLE FORESTRY INITIATIVE

Certified Chain of Custody

Promoting Sustainable Forestry

www.sfiprogram.org

SFI-01268

SFI label applies to text stock

15 16 17 18 19 10 9 8 7 6 5 4 3 2 1

Contents

Preface

Welcome to the Corwin Connected Educators Series.

Last year, Ariel Price, Arnis Burvikovs, and I assembled a great list of authors for the Fall 2014 books in the Corwin Connected Educators Series. As leaders in their field of connected education, they all provided practical, short books that helped educators around the world find new ways to connect. The books in the Spring 2015 season will be equally as beneficial for educators.

We have all seen momentous changes for educators. States debate the use of the Common Core State Standards, and teachers and leaders still question the use of technology, while some of their students have to disconnect and leave it at home because educators do not know how to control learning on devices. Many of the Series authors worked in schools where they were sometimes the only ones trying to encourage use of technology tools at the same time their colleagues tried to ban it. Through their PLNs they were able to find others who were trying to push the envelope.

This spring, we have a list of authors who are known for pushing the envelope. Some are people who wrote books for the Fall 2014 season, while others are brand new to the series. What they have in common is that they see a different type of school for students, and they write about ideas that all schools should be practicing now.

Rafranz Davis discusses *The Missing Voices in EdTech*. She looks at and discusses how we need to bring more diverse voices to the connected world because those voices will enrich how we learn and the way we think. Starr Sackstein, a teacher in New York City writes about blogging for reflection in her book *Blogging for Educators*. Twitter powerhouse Steven W. Anderson returns to the Series to bring us *Content Curation*, as do the very engaging Joseph M. Sanfelippo and Tony Sinanis with their new book, *Principal Professional Development*. Mark Barnes rounds out the comeback authors with his book on *5 Skills for the Global Learner*. Thomas C. Murray and Jeffrey Zoul bring a very practical "how to" for teachers and leaders in their book *Leading Professional Learning*, and Makerspaces extraordinaire Laura Fleming brings her expertise with *Worlds of Making*.

I am insanely excited about this book series. As a former principal I know time is in short supply, and teachers and leaders need something they can read today and put into practice tomorrow. That is the exciting piece about technology; it can help enhance your practices by providing you with new ideas and helping you connect with educators around the world.

The books can be read in any order, and each will provide information on the tools that will keep us current in the digital age. We also look forward to continuing the series with more books from experts on connectedness.

As Michael Fullan has been saying for many years, technology is not the right driver, good pedagogy is, and the books in this connected series focus on practices that will lead to good pedagogy in our digital age. To assist readers in their connected experience, we have created the Corwin Connected Educators companion website where readers can connect with the authors and find resources to help further their experience. The website can be found at www .corwin.com/connectededucators. It is our hope that we can meet you where you are in your digital journey, and bring you up to the next level.

Peter DeWitt, EdD @PeterMDeWitt

About the Authors

 **Thomas C. Murray** serves as the state and district digital learning director for the Alliance for Excellent Education located in Washington, DC. He has testified before the United States Congress and works alongside that body, the US Department of Education and state departments of education, corporations, and school districts throughout the country to implement digital learning while leading Future Ready, Project 24, and Digital Learning Day. Murray's experiences in K–12 digital leadership, which include implementing a 1:1 program, BYOD, blended learning, and a K–12 cyber school where he served as the director of technology and cyber education for the Quakertown Community School District in Bucks County, Pennsylvania, have been recognized nationally.

A former school principal, Murray is passionate about proper digital learning implementation and personalized professional learning. He was the recipient of the Blended Schools Network Leadership Award, named one of the top 16 "forward thinking EdTech leaders in the country," named one of the "top 100 influential voices in education," has been featured in *Tech & Learning* magazine's Leadership Profile, and has appeared on various television shows. Murray's cyber- and blended-learning programs have been highlighted by Forbes.com, *T.H.E. Journal*, *District Administration* magazine, Project Red, *Tech & Learning* magazine, the Innosight Institute, and iNACOL, among others, and on Digital Learning Day in both 2013 and 2014. He also serves on the advisory board for *T.H.E. Journal* and Remind. Murray is the cofounder of #edtechchat, a weekly educational technology

Twitter forum, where hundreds of educators from around the world discuss digital learning. As a follow-up, his weekly show, #edtechchat radio on the BAM Radio Network, is available on iTunes and is regularly one of the top downloaded education podcasts. Connect with him on Twitter @thomascmurray or at www.thomascmurray.com.

Jeffrey Zoul is a lifelong teacher, learner, and leader, currently serving as assistant superintendent for teaching and learning with Deerfield Public Schools District 109 in Deerfield, Illinois. Prior to working in this capacity, Jeff served as a district administrator in Rock Island, Illinois, and a school improvement specialist with Southern Regional Education Board (SREB), the nation's largest and oldest nonprofit school improvement network. Jeff also served as a principal with Forsyth County Schools in Cumming, Georgia, and with North Shore School District 112 in Highland Park, Illinois.

Before serving as an administrator, Dr. Zoul was a classroom teacher for eighteen years in Georgia, teaching elementary school, middle school, and high school English.

Dr. Zoul is also the author of several books, including *Improving Your School One Week at a Time: Building the Foundation for Professional Teaching and Learning* and *The 4 CORE Factors for School Success*, coauthored with Dr. Todd Whitaker. Jeff has also served as an adjunct professor at North Georgia College and State University, teaching graduate-level courses in research and assessment. In 2014, he was awarded the Bammy Educators Voice Award as the School Business Official of the Year.

Dr. Zoul earned a bachelor of arts degree in education from the University of Massachusetts at Amherst and a master of science degree in education from Troy University. In addition, Zoul earned an education specialist's degree from the University of Southern Mississippi and a doctoral degree from the University of Alabama in Tuscaloosa, Alabama. Please connect with Jeff via Twitter @Jeff_Zoul or at http://jeffzoul.blogspot.com.

Introduction

The Need for Systemic Change

It's four o'clock on a typical Thursday afternoon. Teachers begin shuffling in to the latest workshop offered, one listed on the district professional learning calendar. This particular session happens to be on one of the latest technology tools. Some teachers signed up with sincere interest in learning the tool, others because Thursday is the only night they can carve out time after school, while others simply because they needed to log the additional two hours of their professional learning time. Upon arrival, the teachers sign in to verify their attendance so that the workshop hours count and will be recorded. For the next two hours, the group watches the presenter, Marie, share the tool and how she uses it in the classroom and how they, too, can do the same. As the end of the workshop approaches, many teachers begin glancing at their watches, knowing that the two-hour window is almost up and their hours have almost been earned. As the session concludes, the teachers kindly thank their colleague Marie for sharing, say goodnight, and walk out the door to head home.

A few weeks later, just before Thanksgiving break, the teachers begin to congregate at the local middle school for the latest in-service day. Upon arrival, the teachers sign in at the

(Continued)

(Continued)

front door and pick their schedule up for the day. In their packet is the outline of the sessions they'll be going to and the grade-level meetings they'll attend and what time they can leave. The day begins with an hour-long session in the auditorium, where district office representatives talk about the latest initiatives, what the teachers have to do, and how teachers' success will be measured. Over the next six hours, teachers rotate between sessions offering what input they are able to. At the end of the day, it's a stampede out the front door and off for the long weekend.

The scenarios just described are commonplace in school districts across the nation. Teachers sign up for afterschool workshops, often required contractually by a set number of hours, and attend in-service days sporadically spaced throughout the year. In combination, many times these two components encompass a district's professional learning plan.

Some say the definition of insanity is doing the same thing over and over again, while expecting a different result. Realizing this, many districts are changing their approach to professional learning, knowing that the traditional model of top-down, sit-and-get, hours-based professional learning is simply ineffective.

Leading Professional Learning: Tools to Connect and Empower Teachers outlines a different way, a way that cultivates teacher leadership, builds capacity in staff, encourages building leaders to be transparent in their own learning, and develops shared ownership and a culture of learning.

WHAT DO WE CONSIDER "TRADITIONAL" PROFESSIONAL LEARNING?

Traditional professional learning is top-down

In many traditional settings, professional learning originates out of the district office, often by a director of staff development or some curriculum-oriented position. Although having a position at the district level is not inherently bad, such a position can inadvertently spread the notion that professional learning is someone else's job and is something "done to teachers," as opposed to something each teacher actively participates in and owns. In a school-based setting, professional learning is often planned solely by the building administration with minimal teacher input.

Traditional professional learning is one-size-fits-all

Similar to the educational model of the 1980s, many districts continue to use a one-size-fits-all approach to professional learning. The underlying understanding, however, is that teachers learn at different rates, have different learning styles, and possess a wide span of needs. The one-size-fits-all approach to learning doesn't work in the classroom for students, and it certainly doesn't work as a professional learning model for teachers.

Traditional professional learning is hours-based

Staff often get caught up in "what counts," finding themselves asking for permission to attend particular learning activities. Many districts will deny permission for teachers to obtain "credit" for learning activities that are not district supervised. We find it ironic that districts will trust teachers with the lives of children on a daily basis yet often not "trust" them enough to make their own professional learning decisions. Accumulating "seat time," albeit the data point most often measured, is irrelevant when it comes to determining levels of professional growth. When school leaders use seat time as the measurement tool, they're measuring the wrong end of the learner.

Traditional professional learning uses a "sit and get" format

Walk by a traditional professional learning session, and you're bound to see an instructor-centric environment with teachers seated, facing forward, and a facilitator standing up front. It's one that's eerily similar to the traditional model of classroom instruction. At an extreme level, this entails filling an auditorium with teachers and adding a few district office representatives standing up front facilitating for hours on end. Districts that herd teachers like cattle into large rooms, talk at them for a few hours at a time, and call it "professional" learning are modeling poor instructional practice.

Year after year, many districts continue to offer the exact same model of professional learning yet wonder why there's little performance growth, minimal teacher excitement, an increase in absenteeism on in-service days, and a rush out the front door when the "professional development day" ends. Ironically, this model remains widespread in schools around the nation, while districts are simultaneously discussing personalized learning for students.

> Just as a personalized model meets the needs of today's children, a personalized model for professional learning is also needed to meet the various needs of teachers.

The traditional model simply hasn't worked to the extent needed to serve our teachers and, ultimately, our students. It is time for a change, and there is a better way—a way that motivates and empowers teachers, shares ownership, and personalizes professional learning, all while increasing accountability and expectations for all.

A NOTE ABOUT THE ORGANIZATION OF THIS BOOK

This book includes a total of five chapters following this introduction, and the intended audience is both school and district leaders and classroom teachers at all levels. In Chapters 1 through 4, we make the case for a systemic overhaul from traditional models of professional development. In the process, we share examples and resources, including leadership profiles, tool spotlights, concrete illustrations of how teachers can take ownership of their own professional learning, and how districts can support the transformation process. In Chapter 2, we focus on school leaders, who must model the way in this area, serving as lifelong learners themselves and kick-starting transformation in the area of professional learning for all educators. In Chapter 3, we outline six features of this new model for professional learning and suggest many tools and resources available to accompany this design. In Chapter 5, we summarize key points, make a case for the key shifts needed in the area of professional learning, and offer a call to action we believe is both urgent and important for twenty-first century students and teachers.

A New Vision for
Professional Learning

"In the history of education, no improvement effort has ever succeeded in the absence of thoughtfully-planned and well-implemented professional development."

—Thomas Guskey and
Kwang Suk Yoon (2009, p. 497)

As suggested in the opening quote, any serious attempt to improve schools must include, at its core, a plan for improving the ongoing professional learning experiences of the educators who staff them. Todd Whitaker (2003) goes so far as to suggest that there are, ultimately, only two ways to improve any school: hire better teachers and improve the ones who are already there. This is not said with any intent to demean the current teachers at any school; instead, Whitaker is suggesting that to get better, even our very best teachers need to continuously improve—indeed, that is one thing that makes them so great. And, since hiring new teachers tends to be limited to a few each year—at most—for the majority of schools, it behooves us to focus on the second way forward: doing everything in our power to plan for continuous improvement of our professional teaching staff.

Although we agree wholeheartedly with Whitaker and Guskey and Yoon regarding the importance of carefully planned and executed professional learning experiences for educators, we do wish to emphasize a subtle but important distinction between what Guskey and Yoon (2009) refer to as "professional development" and what we refer to as "professional learning." Although this could be considered a mere matter of semantics, we maintain that the distinction is important enough to establish the case for the latter at the outset of this book. As educators, our core business is, quite simply, learning. First and foremost, our responsibility is to ensure high levels of learning for all students we teach. Almost as important, of course, is our own learning as educators. Becoming "developed" or "trained" strikes us as just a bit off-target and almost contrary to our mission of ensuring high levels of learning for all students and staff. Thus, in this book, we refer to professional (and personalized) *learning* experiences as opposed to professional *development*. "Training" teachers to do something may be appropriate to an extent, but a training—or development opportunity—connotes an event teachers attend to obtain a specific skill that they can, in turn, use in scripted ways and in specific settings. To truly affect student learning, teachers must not merely be

> As teachers, our passion is *learning*, not *development*.

"trained"; they must learn deeply in a way that results in the learning being transferred to their own classrooms and shared with other teachers with whom they interact.

Moreover, "professional development" suggests a one-time event or, at best, a series of events, whereas "professional learning" suggests growth that is ongoing, sustainable, continuous, and *personal*.

WHO OWNS THE LEARNING?

In the introduction to this book, we confront the fact that in many schools and school districts, professional learning is owned not by teachers themselves but, rather, school and/or district leaders who control the delivery of professional learning *to* teachers. To create authentic *personalized learning plans* (PLPs), we must shift the primary ownership of the learning from outside to within, from top-down to organic, from those with formal authority, to the intended learners: teachers. We must shift from thinking it is something we do *to* teachers to something we (with their active participation) do *with* them.

Professional learning has often been viewed as something that occurs outside normal work practices, something additional, usually provided by someone from outside our own workplace. However, professional learning is something most teachers and educators do every day: we reflect on our professional practice, work together, and share ideas and resources in an effort to improve student outcomes. We need to harness this learning energy inherent in our daily lives as professional educators into a systematic, integral component of our school cultures.

Successful personalized learning plans for teachers can and should be—as the very name suggests—*personal*, meaning unique to the teacher doing the learning. To truly own their learning, teachers must be learning and experiencing something they find of value and something directly applicable to the work they do, the students they teach, and the content they expect their students to learn. Although this learning, then, can take on a variety of looks, when it occurs as part of the teacher's school day, successful professional learning experiences tend to be those embedded in daily practice, needs-based and linked to student learning needs, tailored to meet the specific circumstances or contexts of participants, and sustained over time. Ideally, creating personalized learning plans for all teachers requires teachers to work collaboratively with school and district leaders to identify where they currently are, what they need next in order to grow, and a plan of action for getting from here to there in order to meet the challenge of ensuring that all students achieve at high levels. A goal of all educators across a district committed to PLPs should be to establish a self-directed, collaborative, and dynamic culture of learning and to build the capability of staff to engage in such a culture of learning. Within such an environment, teachers take control of their own professional learning and integrate it into their daily work lives. Their focus moves from acquiring new knowledge (at best) or enough seat time (at worst), to improving outcomes for students by improving their capability to do so.

Teachers owning their learning is not unlike owning, versus renting, a home. When we move from renting a home to owning one, our investment and responsibility in the process increases dramatically; we no longer live from day-to-day knowing that, ultimately, our home is owned by someone other than us. If something goes wrong, we rely on others to fix it. Once we commit to owning the home ourselves, our level of commitment rises significantly. We maintain it with care, monitor it on a daily basis for anything needing repair, and even plan for opportunities to improve by renovating or expanding when we can. In today's schools, many teachers are merely "renting" the professional learning opportunities offered to them by those who own it; to transform professional learning in our schools, teachers themselves must move from *renting* to *owning* their learning.

TEACHERS AS LEARNERS AND LEADERS

When teachers move from renting to owning their professional learning, they become more invested in it and are more willing to see themselves not only as teachers but also as learners and leaders. How do we intentionally allow for teachers—in collaboration with school and district administrators—to own their learning in this way? We believe that the key to successful personalized learning plans for teachers is to allow for more teacher voice and more teacher choice. To begin listening to teacher voice and designing learning opportunities allowing for teacher choice, school leaders must consider a variety of factors relating to the teachers with whom they work, including the following:

- *Current knowledge and skills.* What is it that teachers already know and can do? How can we build off this current status to move to the next logical level?
- *Motivation.* We must consider teacher motivation for learning. Why are some teachers motivated to learn in one way or learn a certain thing while others prefer (or need) to learn something else or learn in another way? How can we tie teacher learning plans to teacher motivation for learning?
- *Life and career experiences.* Not all teachers are at the same stage of their careers, nor do they arrive with identical life and career experiences. Personalized learning plans take these variables into account when designing and implementing growth opportunities.
- *Beliefs and confidence.* Teachers hold a wide variety of beliefs about teaching and learning and arrive with widely varying levels of confidence in their own ability to not only teach certain concepts or employ certain instructional techniques but also in their ability to learn new concepts or instructional strategies.

To account for these factors related to individual teacher readiness to learn, school leaders must start by finding out where each of our teachers are in their own learning journey and where they think they need to go next in order to grow and improve. We must proactively and directly ask all teachers specific questions about their current knowledge and skillset, their motivation for learning, their past experiences, their beliefs about how they learn best, and their own confidence level in how prepared they are to meet the varying and ever-changing demands of their jobs as professional educators. Prior to the beginning of each school year, school leaders charged with overseeing professional learning must conduct such a needs assessment, surveying all teachers in their school or district about these aspects of professional learning before designing the school or district professional learning plans for the school year. (For an example of such a needs assessment, please visit the Connected Educators companion website.) Throughout the year they must create and deliver a variety of learning opportunities for all staff based on these needs and allowing for *teacher voice* and *teacher choice* about what, how, and when they will learn based on their individual, grade level, department, or team needs. At the end of the year, they must survey teachers again to see if the intended learning targets were actually met and what the next targets must be as the cycle begins anew.

In addition to focusing on teachers as learners, we must also take advantage of the expertise of teachers who have exhibited a capacity for—and expressed a desire for—serving as leaders. We believe that every teacher in every school knows something about his or her craft that another teacher does not. The more we can learn from within by learning from our own experts—the teachers with whom we serve—the more flexible we can be in offering a wide variety of personalized learning opportunities designed to meet the specific needs of our own schools and districts.

In the ensuing chapters of this book, we outline specific types of learning experiences school and district leaders can collaboratively plan, implement, and monitor. Whether we are designing opportunities for teachers to observe each other within their own buildings; allowing teachers to visit other schools to observe what is working elsewhere; grouping teachers with similar needs into professional learning communities; organizing book study groups;

creating opportunities for professional dialogues; establishing mentoring relationships; facilitating virtual learning opportunities via Skype, Twitter, Google Hangouts, Voxer, or other online venues; encouraging attendance at Edcamps; or simply redesigning the precious "official" blocks of professional learning time available to us, we must begin the process by listening to teacher *voice* and then designing a menu of options allowing for *choice*. We need to intentionally plan for voice and choice both in how, when, and what teachers *learn* as well as how, what, and when they *lead* their colleagues in the learning.

Tool Spotlight: Google Forms for Soliciting Teacher Feedback

In this chapter, we emphasize the importance of soliciting teacher input prior to designing any professional learning plans in a school or district. One simple tool all educators can use to gather such feedback is Google Forms. A Google Form is a great resource for gathering information, a fast and simple way to create an online survey, with responses collected onto an online spreadsheet in real time. You can create your survey and invite respondents via e-mail or by sharing the form's web address. Participants can answer questions from almost any web browser—including smartphone and tablet browsers. As people respond, the person who created the form is able to view each response in a single row of a spreadsheet or charts showing the summary of responses. Like many amazing tools available to educators today, Google Forms is not only easy and efficient to use but also free! (To learn more about how to use Google Forms, please visit the Connected Educators companion website.)

NOTE: Google Forms is also an excellent formative assessment tool for classroom use, particularly in a 1:1 and/or BYOD environment. The notion of "every child, every answer, every time" becomes feasible as real-time feedback provides instant, usable data for the classroom teacher.

Michelle Nebel (@MNebel), Excelsior Springs School District, Excelsior Springs, Missouri; chief innovations officer, #moedchat moderator on Twitter, and adjunct professor

Nebel's insights on a new vision for professional learning and her district's road to personalized learning for teachers:

Redefining Professional Learning

In order for our district to transform its previous professional development practices, all stakeholders needed to shift to a new vision of professional learning. Empowered professionals driving their own continuous learning, holding themselves accountable, and focusing on outcomes became the heart of our new vision. The district expanded its definition of what constitutes professional development, when it can happen, how it can be delivered, who can deliver it, and how it is measured. We adopted a variety of professional learning delivery methods that enhanced teacher voice and provided teachers with multiple options allowing them to determine their own path to learning.

Two favorite methods included using an "unconference" format and "speed discussions." *Unconference* refers to a gathering of educators exchanging information and ideas in a less formal structure, allowing participants the opportunity to determine the agenda by creating it themselves at the beginning of the day.

Speed discussions are a series of short conversations, each focusing on a specific topic, usually lasting about ten minutes per topic. Educators self-select which discussions to attend. For instance, one discussion might center on formative assessment and another on an app for creativity; the list of options is limited solely by the interests and needs of the participants.

In order to make professional development as pertinent as possible to each staff member and recognize individual needs, staff members were provided a "flex day." The goal for the day was to provide time for informal learning that was self-organized, self-initiated, just-in-time, and made visible to others. This goal placed teachers in charge of their learning by having them make decisions on what to learn, how to learn it, and how to display their learning for others. These are but a few ways we are striving to redesign teacher learning experiences in our district.

Lead Learners Model the Way

"A leader is one who knows the way, goes the way, and shows the way."

—John C. Maxwell

THE LEADERSHIP GAP

Ever since the advent of No Child Left Behind, we have heard the constant refrain in the United States regarding the need to close the achievement gap that exists among various student populations within our nation's schools. This gap in student achievement remains a real problem in our schools and merits ongoing conversation and debate focused on how best to close the gap. We simply can no longer accept living in a nation in which one's zip code determines one's level of academic achievement. Although addressing this gap may well be our nation's first and foremost priority, we have also noticed another educational gap requiring immediate attention: that in teachers' professional learning in which we, as school leaders, say one thing regarding instruction in our classrooms and do another thing. We maintain that these two gaps of student achievement and professional learning are related, and we will not solve the larger issue until we address the corresponding one.

Over the past two years, we have noticed a significant increase in professional dialogue focusing on the need to personalize learning for students. Although this is welcome news, unfortunately, we have heard and read much less about the need to also personalize learning for teachers; we believe that both conversations are equally important and necessary if we are to increase levels of academic achievement for all students. We must design personalized, meaningful, and practical professional learning plans for every teacher at every school in every school district. As mentioned in the preface, we can no longer rely on top-down, hours-based, one-size-fits-all professional learning models for our nation's teachers. Although one could make a case for this being an *efficient* model of delivery, it is neither efficacious nor what we must model for teachers if we are serious about expecting them to change their own instructional practices. The leadership gap in the area of what we *say* we need to do in the area of professional learning and what we *actually* do is more of a chasm than a gap, and it is every bit as important as the gap we face in student achievement. To address the latter, we must also address the former.

Moving from traditional professional learning in our nation's schools to more personalized professional learning opportunities for our teachers must begin with school leaders. Central office leaders must first model and offer this for principals. Building administrators, in turn, must model and offer this for the teachers in their schools. In Michael Fullan's (2014) most recent book *The*

Principal: Three Keys to Maximizing Impact, he advocates moving from the view that the principal should serve as the *instructional leader* to seeing the principal as the *lead learner* within the school. The distinction is both subtle and powerful. School principals—particularly those serving in large schools with many teachers teaching many grades and/or content areas—cannot be expected to become experts in every area of curriculum, instruction, and assessment. They can, however, serve as the "lead learner" by teaching and modeling—through their words and actions—what they are learning, how they are learning it, and why it matters. Principals who focus on serving as the lead learner, rather than the instructional leader, at the schools in which they serve know that it is vitally important for them to communicate their expectations for all staff members, even outlining specific instructional nonnegotiables that will become part of the school culture. At the same time, they hold even higher expectations for themselves in this area and model what they expect from teachers by living out these behaviors whenever and however they can. As Maxwell wisely suggests in the chapter-opening quote, effective school leaders know the way, show the way, and go the way they want others to follow.

TIME: STOP SPENDING, START INVESTING

Although it is our view that the building principal must model a new approach to professional learning if the ultimate goal is for all staff members to invest in their own learning in a new way, we also realize that the building principal is not the sole leader in any school building. The principal must lead this work and model the way along with, depending on the size of the school, assistant principals, department chairs, instructional coaches, and team leaders. Together, school leaders who wish to transform professional learning for teachers by providing every staff member the opportunity to design and follow a personalized learning plan for continuous improvement begin the process by monitoring their own learning and ensuring that they have a PLP in place for themselves. They share this plan with everyone at the school, modeling the way and inspiring a shared vision for what continuous professional learning should look like, serving, as Fullan suggests (2014), as the lead learners of their school communities.

An obstacle to designing, implementing, and monitoring high-quality, engaging professional learning experiences for all teachers in many schools and districts is a lack of dedicated time for this important aspect of our profession. Typically, schools have no more than a handful of days set aside for professional learning during the course of a school year. Moreover, finding time for professional learning before, during, and after regular school days can be challenging. Even dedicating short amounts of time to professional learning during regularly scheduled meeting times can prove easier said than done. A lack of time amid daily schedules already overflowing with commitments can become a legitimate concern, even for educators passionate about transforming their own learning. Although we suspect there will never be enough time built into any school year to accomplish everything we would like to in terms of personalizing learning for all teachers, we have seen successful practices work in many schools around the nation and strongly believe they can be replicated in any school or district.

Success in creating the necessary time to personalize learning for teachers begins in the same way success in any area often begins: with a shift in our mind-sets. Carol Dweck (2007) has popularized the concept of a *growth mind-set* versus a *fixed mind-set*, suggesting through her research that people who operate from a growth mind-set can accomplish, learn, and grow more than their counterparts who have a fixed mind-set, who believe that their abilities are static and innate. Having a growth mind-set when it comes to improving our practice as educators is essential to our success and, more importantly, to our students' success. Regardless of how expert any teacher currently is, she or he can always become even better. In addition, no two teachers are at the exact same point on any continuum in their current level of expertise in every area of professional practice. Among many teachers of varying proficiency levels in any school district, each individual teacher's "point A" (his or her current proficiency level) is unique. Knowing that teachers are scattered all along this line of proficiency, the goal is not to expect every teacher to get to the exact same point on the spectrum by the end of any single school year. The goal is to make certain that every teacher grows and learns, moving from the teacher's current Point A to his or her personal Point B. Much like the students we serve, teachers are all over the spectrum in their current levels of proficiency on an almost infinite number of professional practices important to both the art and science of teaching.

In addition to adopting a growth mind-set when it comes to personalized learning for teachers, we must also adopt an investment mind-set, as opposed to a spending mind-set. No matter how intentional we are about the way we use time, there will always be precious little available to accomplish all that we must. Therefore, we need to move from merely spending time to investing our time. Traditionally, schools have simply spent their professional learning time by offering whole-group, one-time, episodic events. School leaders spend time scheduling an event and teachers spend a defined amount of time attending the event. When the event is completed, our time is spent and we move forward until the next stand-alone event on which we will spend our precious time and resources. On the other hand, when we actually invest in our teachers and their professional learning, such events take on a different look and feel.

School leaders must make the conscious decision to invest in teachers' professional learning as a long-term commitment that we hope pays off not just today but over a long period of time. This type of investment is different from, say, spending money on textbooks or Smart Boards for classrooms. Such purchases may—or may not—be money well spent, but even assuming the best, these are still merely transactions, spending a specific amount of money to get specific tools or materials to every teacher in the school.

Rather than a series of stand-alone purchases, investing in personalized learning must focus not on a *transaction* but on *transformation*. And this transformation starts by relationship building. School leaders must know their teachers every bit as well as they expect teachers to know their students. They must know their strengths, their areas for growth, their interests, and their experiences. Then, they must work together with each teacher to collaboratively design a personalized learning plan that will meet the teacher's needs. Our expectation is that these investments will take root and grow, providing returns long after we have made them. School leaders with an investment mind-set tend to focus more on spending *time* with their teachers rather than spending *money* on teachers when it comes to personalized learning plans. It may well be easier to spend money than time, since time is such a limited commodity in the life of busy school leaders. Still, leaders with an investment mind-set make the time to invest in this way knowing that—in the long run—the return will be vastly greater than if they had simply spent some money to bring in an outside speaker to work with all staff members at the school for a single day.

In the school setting, investing in others can take many forms. Although our first priority is investing in the students we serve, investing in teachers by offering them the time it takes to become fully aware of their learning needs and determining how to meet them is a close second.

MAKING THE MOST OF FACULTY MEETINGS

School leaders can and should model for others in a variety of ways how they envision professional learning. Frankly, almost anything school leaders say or do is an opportunity to model how they hope others will behave. We focus on two such opportunities: faculty meetings and blogging.

In many schools, faculty meetings are taking on a different look from the traditional faculty meetings in which the entire faculty sat together listening to the principal transmit information. Traditional faculty meetings were rarely targeted as opportunities to focus on professional learning and, instead, were used primarily as information dissemination sessions, a means to share information with all staff members. With a plethora of technology tools now available to transmit this information more effectively and more efficiently, it no longer makes sense to use precious time with the entire faculty to do this. Instead of dedicating faculty meeting time to announcements and managerial information that can simply be communicated through e-mail, principals should model how best to spend staff time together by completely rethinking the purpose of faculty meetings. When school leaders do schedule whole-faculty meetings, they should do so with four purposes in mind:

1. To build relationships among staff members
2. To celebrate school and staff accomplishments
3. To identify problems and brainstorm possible solutions
4. To focus on professional learning

Together, these four purposes for whole-faculty meetings work together to accomplish a still larger goal: creating and maintaining a healthy and positive school culture. The way we approach any meeting we schedule goes a long way in determining what the school culture will look and feel like.

Any time the whole faculty is called together, the entire meeting time should be spent engaged in activities that fulfill one or more of these purposes. Of course, there is other work that must be done during school meetings that falls outside these four purposes, but our experience is that such work need not require the entire faculty gathering at one time in one place. School leaders can schedule team, grade-level, department, and committee meetings to accomplish this other work. Building leaders must be careful to intentionally schedule time for both whole-faculty and smaller team meetings, each with nonnegotiable expectations in place for all meeting attendees. Such nonnegotiables may include the following:

- Any scheduled meeting will have a stated purpose, a clear and viable agenda, and an agreed-on start and stop time.
- Team meeting norms will be established, communicated, monitored, and adhered to by all members.
- Roles and responsibilities for meeting attendees will be clearly outlined and shared among all members.
- The physical setting for each meeting will be conducive to maximizing productivity, including appropriate seating, work spaces, audio-visual capabilities, temperature, and technology.
- The meeting will be a "safe" environment for all in attendance, meaning that different perspectives are not only allowed but valued and expected.
- Minutes from each meeting will be documented and shared with all appropriate staff members.

Whole-faculty meeting time should be reserved for the sole purposes outlined earlier. Such times should be treated as truly precious opportunities to bond as a team, promote the school's culture, celebrate successes, share stories, and learn together. When it comes to whole-faculty meeting times, we believe in a less-is-more approach, meaning that school leaders should not convene regularly scheduled monthly or semimonthly meetings merely because that is the way it has always been done or that is the frequency for which the contract allows. Instead, whole-faculty meetings should be scheduled purposefully and planned meticulously. Many principals find that scheduling only four such meetings each year suffices, gathering together as a whole staff once each quarter. In addition, of course, many other school meetings must occur during which "nuts and bolts" work is completed, but such meetings rarely require every staff member's presence. During "working" meetings, only those directly involved in the work need attend. Regardless of the decision school leaders make regarding how often to hold whole-staff meetings at their school, here are our tips for holding staff meetings:

1. Remind staff members of the school's mission and values.
2. Open and close the meeting with some type of celebration.
3. Plan whole-faculty meeting "rituals" or traditions followed at each meeting, including sharing stories, celebrating accomplishments, highlighting individual and/or team successes, sharing jokes or anecdotes, and providing refreshments.
4. Ensure that many, if not all, staff members play a lead role during some part of the whole-staff meetings.
5. Find ways for as many voices as possible to be heard during the meeting.
6. Make sure that no meeting lasts for more than sixty minutes.
7. Make sure that whole-faculty meetings include a heavy dose of fun.
8. Set a personal goal for each meeting that all teachers will leave the meeting more excited about teaching at the school than when they arrived.
9. Allow time for staff members to share personal, as well as professional, successes, joys, sorrows, and challenges. Create a culture of caring among staff members that extends beyond the schoolhouse.
10. Spend ten to twenty minutes of each whole-staff meeting modeling the way as "lead learner." Do this by "teaching" the staff something you have recently learned through your own personalized learning plan.

A multitude of technology tools enable us to have faculty members participate actively during faculty meetings just like our students do in classrooms. A few such examples include Poll Everywhere, Kahoot.it, Socrative, Soap Box, Edmodo, and TodaysMeet. Each of these services offers free, nonthreatening ways for staff members to actively participate in faculty meeting discussions. While each comes with its own unique advantages and features, we highlight one such tool, TodaysMeet, next.

Time is a precious commodity in our schools, and it seems as if we have less and less with each passing year. School leaders dedicated to personalizing learning for the teachers they serve know one thing, though: they will never *find* the time needed to do so; instead, they *make* the time needed to do so. There simply is no extra time available to find, but by prioritizing what is most important, we can make the time to do what is necessary. Although it may not be necessary to meet as a whole faculty quite as frequently as we have in the past, it remains very important that we do so periodically and that, when such meetings are scheduled, school leaders do everything in their power to ensure that the time is used intentionally. Whole-faculty meeting time should be reserved for relationship building, culture building, problem solving, story sharing—and, of course, professional learning.

Tool Spotlight: TodaysMeet

Backchanneling refers to the conversation that is secondary to the primary conversation being led by a teacher, speaker, principal, or anyone else facilitating a meeting of any type. Backchanneling allows the participants in the audience to weigh in on what is being discussed, providing feedback and asking questions. Several technology tools allow for backchanneling during such events. One such tool we have used often and seen many other educators and presenters use is TodaysMeet. TodaysMeet is a backchannel chat platform for classroom teachers and learners. Designed for teachers, TodaysMeet has in place safeguards that respect the needs and privacy of students while giving educators the tools to encourage and elicit their students' voice in the classroom. Participants join easy-to-start chat rooms instantaneously, with no sign-up, and can immediately engage in powerful conversations that augment the traditional classroom or meeting. Ideas can be curated and rooms can be open for up to a year. As easy and effective as this tool is for teachers to use in the classroom, it is equally easy and appropriate for school leaders to use when meeting with teachers.

To learn more about TodaysMeet, visit their website at: https://todaysmeet.com.

BLOGGING TO LEAD, BLOGGING TO LEARN

Lead learners model the way they expect teachers to facilitate learning with their students by leading faculty meetings in effective, efficient, meaningful, and respectful ways. Leaders also model the way for teachers by blogging. Through blogging, lead learners model a host of traits, behaviors, mind-sets, and habits that they want all educators to consider important, among them:

- The importance of taking a risk by publicly sharing their thoughts in writing.
- The importance of writing in authentic ways and the belief that we should all engage in writing, not just our students.
- The importance of reflecting on their daily lives as educators, sharing what they experience and what they learn from these experiences.
- The importance of communicating regularly with the students, educators, parents, and citizens living in the school community.
- The importance of sharing their stories with the larger educational community as a way to highlight the many good things that are occurring, including spotlighting teachers at their schools who are experiencing success with their students.

Blogging has become an authentic, relevant, and engaging classroom activity in many schools around the globe. Increasing numbers of classrooms we have visited in recent years are taught by teachers who blog and who, in turn, inspire students of all ages to actively blog for real-world audiences. Whereas students previously wrote for an audience of one (their teacher) with their work then posted on the refrigerator, they now have the opportunity to write for an audience of millions (the entire world) with their work posted online. Having students blog is not simply a fun activity; it is also a perfect way for teachers to have their students read and write in ways aligned to Common Core standards. If we want more teachers to engage their students in real-world, Common Core–aligned reading and writing activities, school leaders need to model the way by blogging themselves and sharing their blog posts with not only their school community but also the entire world.

We realize that school leaders are already extremely busy people and that blogging regularly does take time. Yet we feel that this is another example of investing, as opposed to spending, their limited time. The returns we have seen principals realize from this investment once they commit to blogging regularly make a compelling case for all principals and school leaders to follow suit. There are hundreds of school leaders around the world whose blogs we read regularly and inspire us in our own work. We invited a few to share their thoughts on blogging, including why they blog. If you are an educator in any role, we hope that you will be inspired to start (or continue) blogging regularly after reading these insights from educators whose blogs are among the most widely read in the entire education community. We also recommend that you subscribe to these leaders' blogs, as a way to continuously learn and grow. Whether you write blog posts weekly, every other week, or monthly, commit to sharing your story. We suspect you will find this investment of time and effort well worth it!

George Couros (@gcouros on Twitter). George is the division principal for Parkland School Division in Stony Plain, Alberta, and a teaching, learning, and leadership consultant. George posts his thoughts about all aspects of education regularly on his blog *The Principal of Change* available at http://georgecouros.ca/blog.

Couros on blogging: "For me, blogging goes beyond reflection to the point of 'open reflection.' Writing for yourself is powerful, but when you know that an audience can read it, it helps to clarify your own thinking while also creating opportunities for collaboration. If every educator did this type of reflection, we would see monumental shifts in practice."

Ben Gilpin (@benjamingilpin). Ben is the principal at Warner Elementary School in Spring Arbor, Michigan. Ben posts his reflections of teaching, learning, and leading on his blog *The Colorful Principal* available at http://colorfulprincipal.blogspot.com.

Gilpin on blogging: "During the winter of my first year as principal I hit a low point; I didn't feel as though I was communicating and connecting with staff well. It was then that I stumbled onto Twitter and the world of blogging. I have found blogging to be a vehicle for clarification, reflection, and most importantly, increased collaboration. I strongly encourage educators to blog. Even though you may be thinking, 'Who will want to read my blog?' I recommend simply beginning your blogging journey by blogging for yourself, using it to reflect and grow as a person."

Vicki Davis (@coolcatteacher). Vicki is a teacher at Westwood Schools in Camilla, Georgia. She is host of the biweekly *Every Classroom Matters* show on the BAM Radio Network. Vicki's blog, *The CoolCat Teacher*, can be accessed at www.coolcatteacher.com.

Davis on blogging: "In 2005 I sat at my desk feeling like I was behind on new technology. Blogging was the 'new thing' and I had to learn how so I could help my students. I decided that I could write from the perspective of a beginner because I knew I had so much to learn and perhaps that would help other beginners like me. I thought that documenting all of the things I learned might help other busy teachers who were stretched for time and it might save some for them. My first post was titled, 'Wiki Wiki Teaching.' Within months, I had a new community of colleagues who encouraged and taught me. Now, almost ten years later, I have two books, a popular Internet radio show, and Tweet daily, but I am still happily in the classroom. Every day I learn from the Tweets and blogs of other educators and share some of my own. Blogging changed everything in my life and made me a better teacher and *that* is the coolest thing about blogging."

Pernille Ripp (@pernilleripp). Pernille teaches seventh grade in Wisconsin and is the creator of the Global Read Aloud. She posts frequent musings about her life as a teacher at her blog *Blogging Through the Fourth Dimension* available at http://pernillesripp.com.

Ripp on blogging: "I never tell educators to blog. Blogging can be incredibly stressful, hurtful, and invasive at times, yet I always tell people to reflect on what they are doing. However, educators who do choose to blog their reflections then know that their words may plant a seed of change for someone else. That your words may make a world of difference to others, that your life may be changed, enriched, and deepened, just because of your blog. You blog not for others but because your heart and mind tells you to and you realize that your words have power, that others may listen. You blog because you want to and then you hang on for the ride."

Eric Sheninger (@e_sheninger). Eric served as principal at nationally renowned New Milford High School in Bergen County, New Jersey, and serves as a senior fellow at the International Center for Leadership in Education (ICLE), a division of Scholastic. Eric is the author of *Digital Leadership: Changing Paradigms for Changing Times*. Readers can follow Eric's popular blog, *A Principal's Reflections*, at http://esheninger.blogspot.com.

Sheninger on blogging: "Blogging is a powerful way for educators to not only reflect upon professional practice, but also discover and learn from the work of innovative educators across the globe. When I began blogging in 2010, my sole purpose for doing so was to take control of public relations at my school. By sharing best practices and the work of my staff, our stakeholders were constantly in the know, and major media outlets began to take notice as well. Whether using blogs for communications, public relations, or professional learning consistency, a sound message, citing sources, and proofreading are key. The most important element, though, is to weave in actionable experiences into your personal thoughts and opinions."

Tool Spotlight: Edublogs, Blogger, WordPress

There are a number of blogging platforms educators use to share their musings on teaching, learning, leadership, and life as they know it with the entire world. Each platform is similar in many ways, yet each has its own unique tools and features. We have worked with hundreds of educators who blog regularly, most of whom use one of the three blog platforms we highlight here as teacher tools to consider.

Edublogs. This is the world's most popular education blogging service. Edublogs lets you easily create and manage student and teacher blogs, quickly customize designs, and include videos, photos, and podcasts. Edublogs is powered by WordPress; however, its focus and features are geared toward the education community. It is easy, safe, and secure and offers both free and paid options.

To learn more about Edublogs, visit http://edublogs.org.

Blogger. This free weblog publishing tool from Google for sharing text, photos, and video is possibly the most user-friendly blogging platform out there. You can set up as many blogs as you want directly from your Google account.

To learn more about Blogger, visit https://support.google.com/blogger/answer/1623800?hl=en.

WordPress. WordPress is another popular blogging service. Although relatively easy to use, it is clearly aimed at those who are willing to spend time learning its features and can handle an occasionally confusing interface. It offers a wider range of tools for adding content, more widgets than most blogging platforms, excellent social networking integration, and superior customization options.

To learn more about WordPress, visit https://wordpress.com.

Richard Byrne, a former high school social studies teacher who is now best known for his blog *Free Technology for Teachers*, compares these three blogging services here: www.freetech4teachers.com/2008/12/choosing-blogging-platform-and-why-i.html#.U-4EpfldWQf.

Leadership Profile

Jimmy Casas (@casas_jimmy), principal of Bettendorf High School, Bettendorf, Iowa, and moderator of #iaedchat

Casas's insights on how lead learners model the way:

What we model is what we get. These seven words have been the mantra that drives my work as an educational leader for the last twenty-plus years. I recognize and understand the value of supporting and developing our teaching staff. As leaders, we must not forget the importance of supporting the individual growth of our teachers by providing an environment that encourages innovation and risk taking if we aim to build a community of leaders where everyone's talents are appreciated and valued.

As a leader, I cannot expect teachers to do anything I am not willing to do myself when it comes to pushing my own growth as an educator, so I made the decision to become a more connected learner in order to grow as a leader by surrounding myself with other talented educators, acquiring resources to share with my staff, and giving back to others in order to support their learning.

Our leadership team works diligently to provide authentic learning experiences for our staff as part of their professional development by encouraging and supporting them to take ownership for their own learning and growth. We do this through a variety of methods, but all of them are deeply rooted in the belief that the expertise we need is often right here in our own school community. We utilize our own teacher experts to deliver our site-based professional learning in a variety of ways—individual, small groups, teams, etc. We gather input to plan and develop in-services in which teachers drive their own learning. We have hosted other schools on professional learning days, given teachers time to do site visits to other schools and businesses, and even coordinated overnight teacher exchanges with other schools in order to support teacher learning and development. We created a weekly staff blog as a forum for staff to share their stories and to bring our team closer together. We strive to personalize the learning in our school, not just for students, but also for teachers.

Lead learners model the way, but they cannot do it alone. The work we do on behalf of students, teachers, and families is too great for any one person to take on. The best school leaders recognize this and empower their teams in order to build the necessary capacity to strive for greatness!

Personalized Learning
Plans in Action

EMPOWER STAFF TO
DESIGN THEIR OWN LEARNING

In a traditional model, teachers are often left feeling as though professional learning is something done to them, not something of which they are a vital part. Teacher voice in professional learning is imperative yet something largely ignored in many school districts. In a truly "professional" environment, districts empower teachers to design their own learning, and, in turn, teachers take ownership of the learning and are responsible for personal learning outcomes.

When district professional learning plans focus on a set number of hours of seat time as a desired outcome, teachers will follow suit and compile the requested hours, often in a checklist form. The number of hours (often submitted at an end-of-year evaluation conference) becomes the focus, not what was learned in the process and how classroom instruction was transformed. The mind-set of "just tell me what I need to do" or "I have to do four more hours" can be symptomatic of a traditional model. The premise in this type of traditional environment is that all teachers need the same type and amount of professional learning; however, common sense and experience tell us otherwise.

As districts empower teachers to design their own learning and begin to respect nontraditional forms of professional learning, as opposed to focusing on "what hours count," a cultural shift and transformation regarding who owns the learning can be unleashed. In schools where staff are told that conversations on social media or attending Edcamps don't "count" as learning, educators are dissuaded from taking ownership of their own learning. When professional learning conversations are focused on a set number of hours and not on personalized learning outcomes, there is little incentive for educators to seek out their own learning experiences. However, when empowered and encouraged to design their own learning, educators can and do realize personal and cultural transformation.

DESIGNING THE PERSONALIZED ROADMAP

Personalized roadmaps can take a myriad of forms and should be customized to meet the needs and demographics of a particular school or district. Similar to how GPS calculates, predicts, and outlines a pathway to a particular destination, so too should a personalized roadmap for professional learning. As with any travel destination, there are times where detours need to be considered, new pathways need to be found, and recalculating is needed to achieve the journey's final destination. As with any journey, one's starting point determines how long it takes to arrive at the final destination. These all hold true when designing personalized plans.

Personalized plans for professional learning contain the following components:

- Teacher voice is at the heart of the plan's roadmap.
- Seat time is irrelevant. The learning outcome is what matters most.
- Professional learning occurs in both formal and informal environments.
- Nontraditional forms of professional learning (e.g., blogging, social media, Twitter chats, Edcamps) are recognized as valuable learning experiences.
- Teachers are responsible for learning outcomes and must be able to communicate how their learning has improved their craft; specifically, how their personal growth has improved classroom experiences for students.
- A supervisor's input is a vital part of the plan, yielding a collaboratively designed roadmap for professional growth.

EXPANDING BOUNDARIES

Much of high-quality personalized professional learning happens outside the walls of a school and far past the boundaries of any given school district. Each day, educators are taking charge of their own learning through connections on social media. From networking with others worldwide, to taking part in weekly chats on Twitter, to sharing resources on Pinterest, to connecting through groups on Facebook, nontraditional forms of professional learning offer educators the ability to connect with others and design their own personalized roadmap for learning. This sweeping movement of professional learning, and those taking part—educators who are often referred to as "connected educators"—have broken down traditional barriers while expanding and flattening possibilities for all. Connected educators collaborate both online and in person, use social media to interact with educators around the world, engage in conversations in online spaces, and most importantly bring their learning back to their home environment to transform the learning space. Educators connecting in these spaces often refer to these connections as their *personal* learning network or PLN.

Twitter

Many educators are connecting on Twitter, an online social microblogging platform, where conversation bites (tweets) are limited to 140 characters at a time. Educators share research articles and blog posts, discuss issues and trends, and engage in healthy, professional debate. Twitter is one of the most popular online mediums in which educators connect worldwide. While connected on Twitter, educators use a compilation of hashtags to crowdsource resources and engage in online conversation regarding everything from educational technology trends, to Common Core resources and implementation, to instructional best practices.

The Role of Hashtags

A hashtag is a word or phrase preceded by the pound symbol (#) and is a way to aggregate particular themes or topics using various social media tools such as Twitter, Facebook, and Instagram. Anyone can use or start a particular hashtag, and using such a hashtag makes the social media content public for the world to see. Educators are using hashtags on a daily basis to brand their school, connect with others on a similar interest or topic, and to share resources. Some popular hashtags include #edchat (education chat), #edtech (educational technology), and #highered (higher education).

At the school and district level, leaders are using hashtags to share school news, collaborate, build school culture, and share resources. In Fall Creek, Wisconsin, Superintendent Joe Sanfelippo has used the #gocrickets hashtag to share his district's story with the community. On a daily basis, resources are shared, classroom learning is highlighted, and the community is engaged with the goings-on of Fall Creek School District through this social media hashtag. This captivating branding has helped to transform a district's culture to one that is collaborative and growth-oriented while simultaneously building school pride and engaging the community.

Using Twitter Chats for Professional Learning

Each week, educators from around the world take part in various conversations on Twitter known as "chats." As of this writing, well over 300 education chats occur weekly. These conversations have become an excellent way for educators to connect on relevant topics and themes, all while challenging each other's thinking. The premise of a Twitter chat is simple. Each chat lasts for sixty minutes, with moderators posing questions on a predetermined topic and participants using a consistent hashtag (#) to communicate. Here's an example from a parent-teacher chat (#ptchat):

Joe Mazza 🐦
@Joe_Mazza
QUESTION 6 - How can parents and teachers involve their school secretaries in planning school functions & events? #ptchat

Questions are posed in a sequential (e.g., Q1, Q2) format over the sixty-minute time period. Participant responses follow the same format, beginning with "A1," "A2" (Answer 1, 2), and so on, to indicate the question to which a participant is responding. For example,

Dana Sirotiak 🐦
@ Sirotiak02
A6. Involve secretaries with important functions such as Open House, B2BN, Report Card, Parent Conferences. #ptchat

Note the #ptchat hashtag embedded in each tweet, curating these tweets into the same stream of information. A variety of tools such as Tweetdeck, HootSuite, and Tweetchat can be used to aggregate the chat into a single stream to ease the conversation process. Taking it one step further, Storify (www.storify.com) allows users to curate and share the compiled information. Chat facilitators will often Storify the conversation and share for use at a later time.

Tool Spotlight: TweetDeck

TweetDeck (https://tweetdeck.twitter.com), owned by Twitter, is an online resource that helps users aggregate the steady flow of information coming to them. It's available as a website, as an app on a smartphone, or as an app in Google Chrome. Users can organize and build custom timelines and keep track of user identified lists, searches, specific hashtags, mentions, and more. The interface allows users to customize the information viewed, therefore personalizing the communication and ultimately the learning.

The following highlights some of the most popular Twitter chats in three main areas.

General Education Chats
#Edchat

The first of the educational chats, conversations in this chat surround a myriad of education topics and trends. Participants vote on the weekly topics, which have ranged from blended learning, to the value of homework, to spicing up faculty meetings, to high-quality professional learning and many more. Founded by Tom Whitby (@tomwhitby), Steven Anderson (@web20classroom), and Shelly Terrell (@shellterrell), this chat occurs Tuesdays from noon to 1:00 p.m. and 7:00 to 8:00 p.m. EST and is one of the most popular education chats found today.

#Satchat

Similar to #edchat, #satchat conversations encompass a variety of educational topics and trends. From professional learning to branding your school, this chat covers all aspects of effective educational practices. Moderated by Scott Rocco (@scottrrocco), Brad Currie (@bcurrie5), and Bill Krakower (@wkrakower), this chat occurs Saturdays from 7:30 to 8:30 a.m. EST and 7:30 to 8:30 a.m. PST.

Theme-Related Chats

#PTchat

The Parent-Teacher Chat (#PTchat) is a weekly social media professional learning conversation that enables parents, family engagement practitioners, teachers, school leaders, and others challenged in this area to develop new and innovative approaches to school-family partnerships. Founded by Joe Mazza (@Joe_Mazza), Gwen Pescatore (@gpescatore25), and Dana Sirotiak (@dsirotiak), this chat occurs Wednesdays from 9:00 to 10:00 p.m. EST. As a follow-up, during the summer, #ptchat evolved into #ptcamp, a virtual summer professional learning experience focused on a different book for six weeks from June through the first week in August. Check out iel.org/ptchat for all past archives, and follow hashtags #parentcamp, #ptcamp, and #ptchat for thousands of free, PLN-based resources at your disposal.

#Edtechchat

On a weekly basis, hundreds of educators come together to discuss all things related to educational technology. From Google Apps for Education, apps for classroom instruction, and technology-supported professional learning, to breaking down barriers for technology integration, this is one of the most popular weekly chats. Founded by Tom Murray (@thomascmurray), Susan Bearden (@s_bearden), Katrina Stevens (@katrinastevens1), Alex Podchaski (@ajpodchaski), and Sharon Plante (@iplante), this chat occurs on Monday nights from 8:00 to 9:00 p.m. EST.

#Ntchat

Founded by Lisa Dabbs (@teachingwthsoul), New Teacher Chat was created to provide weekly mentoring and focus on the needs of teachers new to the profession and preservice teachers worldwide. The chat is supportive and practitioner focused. #ntchat occurs on Wednesday nights from 8:00 to 9:00 p.m. EST.

State Chats

#EdchatRI

Edchat Rhode Island is moderated by Don Miller (@dmiller212001) and Alan Tenreiro (@alantenreiro) and occurs Sundays from 8:00 to 9:00 p.m. EST. For this chat, educators have joined together to discuss education in the Ocean State; however, educators from all over the world usually join the conversation. The focus of this chat is on teachers and administrators sharing best practices both in the classroom and in districts as a whole.

#IAedchat

In November 2012, Jimmy Casas (@casas_jimmy), Matt Degner (@mwdegner), and Aaron Becker (@aaron_becker32) started #IAedchat (Sundays, 8:00–9:00 p.m. CST) as a way to bring Iowa educators and others from across the globe together on a weekly basis to discuss educational topics of interest with educators. In the span of one year, the following had grown so large that #IAedchat leaders decided to add another weekly time slot in order to take the conversation to a deeper level and try to expand the chat to an even wider audience. With the overwhelming growth of this state chat, three additional Iowa educators joined the team, Shannon Miller (@shannonmmiller), Dan Butler (@danpbutler), and Devin Schoening (@dschoening). With these additions came some changes, including an additional weekly time slot (Sundays, 8:00–9:00 a.m. CST) and a monthly recorded live show with special guests.

Twitter chats have evolved into an excellent, personalized form of professional learning where any educator—from superintendents and those at the state level, to the first-year teacher new to the classroom—can take ownership of his or her own learning. On a weekly basis, thousands of educators are sharing their insights, soliciting feedback, and getting connected. You can, too.

Tool Spotlight: Weekly Twitter Chat Schedule

Interested in taking part in a chat but not sure where to start? The Weekly Twitter Chat Schedule can be found at bit.ly/officialchatlist and highlights more than 300 chats that occur weekly. Some chats, such as #sschat, are subject specific, others, such as #4thchat and #kinderchat, are grade-level specific, while others, such as #USedchat, are more general. These chats provide meaningful, engaging opportunities for educators to connect with others around the world with similar interests.

Pinterest

Pinterest is another popular technology tool many educators use for personalized professional learning. Erin Klein (@kleinerin), 2014 MACUL K–12 Teacher of the Year (Michigan), shares the following about using Pinterest as a professional learning tool:

> At its core, Pinterest is a social bookmarking tool that allows users to save their favorite resources. Because of the ease of use and visually appealing interface, educators have gravitated towards this platform to save, share, and collaborate. I've seen various creative ways teachers are utilizing the tool to support and enhance their practice. One of my favorite ways to use Pinterest is by taking advantage of their collaborative board features.
>
> Collaborative Pinterest boards allow multiple users to Pin content to the same board without having to share an

account. Simply have one user set up a board and add the other contributors via their Pinterest handle or via e-mail address. Once each person is added to the board, users can add content the same as they would from their individual accounts. The collaborative board is then added to their collection of independent boards. So, when adding a new Pin, or saving new content, the collaborative board will populate as a choice for boards to save to. Users will be able to see the content they've saved along with the resources other contributors have Pinned to that board.

Pinterest has enabled our team to truly grow professionally on an individual level and brought us together on a professional level. Of course, the best part is that our students are the ones who reap these benefits, and it doesn't get better than that!

The UnConference—Edcamp

Kristen Swanson (@kristenswanson), one of the founders of the Edcamp movement, shares her insight into how Edcamps can play a role in professional learning opportunities for educators:

Edcamps are free, organic professional learning opportunities by teachers, for teachers. Any educator can hold a session at an Edcamp, and the schedule is determined on the day of the event in response to the most cutting-edge, pressing needs of the group. Based on open space technology, Edcamp events are derived from the belief that a group of people, given a purpose and freedom, have the ability to self-organize, self-govern, and produce results. Educators who attend Edcamps are treated as experts, and an open exchange of learning and sharing takes place.

EDCAMPS ARE

- Free
- Non-commercial and with a vendor free presence
- Hosted by any organization or anyone

- Made up of sessions that are determined on the day of the event
- Events where anyone who attends can be a presenter
- Reliant on the law of two feet that encourages participants to find a session that meets their needs

Edcamp empowers educators and changes the paradigm of professional learning.

PROFESSIONAL RESOURCES

Edutopia (www.edutopia.org)

Elana Leoni, director of social media strategy and marketing for Edutopia, shares the following:

> Edutopia, produced by the George Lucas Educational Foundation, offers free resources for anyone wanting to improve education. You'll find a variety of blog posts and articles focused on particular topics such as project-based learning, technology integration, classroom management, and more. Additionally, an extensive video library that showcases evidence-based learning practices and a robust community of education change-makers are readily available. Make sure to check out their flagship series, "Schools That Work," which highlights practices and case studies from K–12 schools and districts that are improving the way students learn.

EdSurge (www.edsurge.com)

EdSurge is a leading site for educators, entrepreneurs, and investors involved in education technology. EdSurge works to discover the best products and ideas for students across the nation and helps educational technology creators understand what classrooms and teachers need to accomplish high levels of success. Curriculum products, teacher needs, school operations, and postsecondary education are just a few of the categories where relevant, up-to-date information and ideas can be found.

edWeb (edWeb.net)

Lisa Schmucki, founder and CEO of edWeb.net, relates the organization's mission:

> edWeb.net's mission is to provide educators with an easy, fun, and free way to get personalized professional learning. We host professional learning communities that host free webinars (live and archived) on thirty-five innovative topic areas and provide CE certificates to any educator who attends or views one of our webinars. edWeb is perfect for an individual teacher and also for school leaders and PD coordinators to provide access to a wide range of PD where educators can follow their own professional learning path. Rachel Langenhorst, technology integrationist, sums it up best: "When you have teachers and people in my position who are planning PD, and can do it in a way that is meaningful to each and every teacher, in any content area—it's really exciting, because it's easy to get onto, easy to work, and everyone can take away something and share with someone else. To me that's absolutely an immeasurable quality."

eSchool News (www.eschoolnews.com)

From the eSchool News staff:

> For the last 17 years, eSchool News has been a go-to source of daily ed-tech news and information for K–12 educators and administrators. The publication's website, www.eschoolnews .com, publishes 2–4 original stories each business day. These stories include news reports on the latest ed-tech trends and innovations, as well as advice on how to use technology to transform instruction and improve school leadership. What's more, the eSchool News website offers free webinars, white

papers, and other resources to help K–12 leaders innovate and solve their biggest challenges with the help of technology. Educators can sign up to receive free daily or weekly e-mail newsletters, as well as a print/digital news magazine that is published several times per year.

SmartBrief
(www.smartbrief.com/industry/education)

SmartBrief packages ten to twelve handpicked articles daily for highly targeted audiences. Educators can receive these daily compilations and customize their reading based on areas of interest. Founded in 1999, the company's premise is simple: there's too much information out there and too little time to read it all. Targeted briefs include resources for language education, educational technology, K–12, leadership, literacy, STEM, special education, and more. This highly respected resource offers an easy way to stay up-to-date on the current issues and trends in education.

BAM Radio Network
(www.bamradionetwork.com)

Errol St. Claire, cofounder, CEO, and executive producer of the BAM Radio Network, shares the following:

> BAM Radio is a network of radio programs hosted by educators for educators, that provides highly personalized professional learning. Educators can choose to listen to educator discussions on over 2,200 topics on 26 channels. Each program features educators discussing a wide range of topics including project-based learning, classroom management, student voice, the maker movement, and educational technology, to name a few.

> Developed for busy educators, BAM Radio is a source for high quality professional learning on the go. Each radio segment runs 8–12 minutes, is available on demand and can be downloaded to allow educators to listen wherever, whenever.

Laura Fleming (@nmhs_lms), library media specialist at New Milford High School, New Milford, New Jersey

Laura's story exemplifies the power of personalized professional learning through the use of digital badges. As the school's technology integration specialist, Laura wanted to create a system in which her colleagues would be given credit for their informal learning. As a result, she created a digital badge–based professional learning platform called Worlds of Learning @ New Milford High School (www.worlds-of-learning-nmhs.com).

Worlds of Learning @ New Milford High School provides a framework that allows teachers, not only at New Milford High School but all around the world, to earn digital badges through learning about technology, tools, and applications and applying their learning to their

classroom instruction to improve learning outcomes. This platform is a place where teachers can learn, experiment, grow, and be challenged.

After registering, teachers can earn badges by learning about a digital learning tool and then demonstrating how they have successfully integrated it into their instruction. Their skill mastery is acknowledged with a digital badging system. They can then showcase their knowledge by displaying their digital learning badges through Credly, the free web service for issuing, learning, and sharing badges or as a Mozilla OpenBadge. From there, their badges can be embedded into their sites or blogs and pushed out to their social networks, or even just printed out and displayed proudly on their classroom walls and doors, as many have done.

REGISTER/LOG IN VIEW BADGES CHOOSE A TASK EARN A BADGE SHOWCASE YOUR ACHIEVEMENT

Teachers can take control of their own professional learning by picking and choosing the skills they want to gain. By flipping their professional learning, teachers receive job-embedded coaching and will be supported by face-to-face, personalized support. New Milford High School teachers have been, and will continue to be, able to take the tools presented in this platform and seamlessly integrate them into meaningful learning that addresses the standards in their respective content areas. The purpose of this platform is to track, share, celebrate and give credit for informal learning.

Developing the Twenty-First Century Professional Learning Mind-Set

As teachers begin to take ownership of their own learning, a shift in mind-set occurs. The professional learning paradigm is no longer a set number of calendar days per year, periodic series of events, or number of hours to obtain. Educators with a twenty-first century professional learning mind-set exemplify the notion that personalized, professional learning is collaborative, engaging, and meaningful.

PROFESSIONAL LEARNING IS COLLABORATIVE

Lev Vygotsky (1962), a Russian teacher and psychologist, first introduced the notion that learning was social in 1962, when he proposed that we learn through our interactions and communications with others. Vygotsky went on to examine how our social environments undoubtedly influence the learning process itself, something many teachers wrestle with—especially while setting up the classroom for a new school year. Vygotsky's theory of social learning suggests that learning takes place through the interactions students have with their peers, teachers, and other experts. Vygotsky's theory that learning is social holds true for adults as well, and this collaborative learning is one key to high-quality, personalized professional learning. As teachers work to create a learning environment that maximizes the learner's ability to interact with others through discussion, collaboration, and feedback, so too can adults create their own personalized learning environment built on this same framework.

Today's teachers with a twenty-first century mind-set are learning collaboratively in unprecedented ways. Examples include the following:

- Engaging conversations at an Edcamp
- A shared board on Pinterest highlighting resources and best practices
- A Twitter chat on an educational hot topic
- A grade-level team's data meeting focused on student learning strategies
- Teacher-facilitated professional learning activities
- Online coursework with a high-quality learning community
- Peer coaching
- A book study with colleagues
- Professional learning communities (PLCs)

JOB-EMBEDDED PROFESSIONAL LEARNING AND THE ROLE OF COACHING

Recognizing the need for modeling and collaborative learning, many districts today are implementing peer coaching as a professional learning strategy. Although this approach may look different in districts across the nation, we believe that teachers working alongside a highly effective coach in the classroom is one of the most powerful forms of professional learning. This type of job-embedded professional learning provides teachers with an opportunity to interact with a master teacher in the environment closest to the student. Follow-up conversation and dissecting what was observed are often the most beneficial aspects of this type of learning. This coaching model moves professional learning from an out-of-the-classroom experience to one that is part of the teacher's daily work—ground zero for their student interactions. Depending on the district's model, coaches may do the following:

- Observe teachers in the classroom and offer specific, personalized feedback
- Facilitate professional learning activities
- Team teach lessons in an effort to model a particular skill
- Help teachers assess students' learning needs and map out strategies for success in meeting these needs

In the same way effective teachers focus on the growth of each student, effective coaches focus on personalized teacher growth and the teacher's instructional transformation and pedagogical shift. In many districts, this type of personalized plan goes hand-in-hand with the development of professional learning communities.

PROFESSIONAL LEARNING COMMUNITIES (PLCs)

Although there is no single definition of a professional learning community (PLC), they tend to focus on two main concepts:

1. Improving the skills and knowledge of educators through collaborative study, expertise exchange, and professional dialogue
2. Improving the educational aspirations, achievement, and attainment of students through stronger leadership and teaching ("Professional Learning Community," 2014, para. 3)

PLCs come in many shapes and sizes and are customized to meet the needs of each school or district implementing this format. Also commonly referred to as collaborative learning groups, critical friends, communities of practice, professional learning groups, whole-faculty study groups, and other descriptors, these groups are typically composed of four to eight team members who meet on a regular basis and quite often include some form of action research as a way to reevaluate and refine the group's predetermined goals for improving teaching and learning. Group norms typically structure the guided conversation.

Richard DuFour, a leader on this topic, describes PLCs as "educators committed to working collaboratively in ongoing processes of collective inquiry and action research to achieve better results for the students they serve" (DuFour, DuFour, Eaker, & Many, 2006, p. 2). Depending on the shared purpose of the PLC, some teams will analyze and reflect on student work, collaborate on instructional best practices, dissect student data and develop action plans for growth, or review literature and develop plans for implementation. Regardless of how this type of experience is named, at the heart of PLCs is professional growth laser-focused on improving instructional practice. At their best, these critical conversations are personalized, and educators' philosophies and instructional practices are transformed at the classroom level.

Breaking Down Traditional District Barriers

One obvious but often overlooked downside of a traditional professional learning model is that a teacher's learning experience is often dictated by the geographical boundaries of his or her given school district. A mere highway may separate what is available and the quality of professional learning that takes place. Simply put, a twenty-first century professional learning mind-set removes geographical barriers. When professional learning is ongoing and systemic, and educators connect with other educators and resources outside their home school district, these traditional barriers of time and location are removed.

Districts teaming up to offer professional learning across a region is another current trend helping to personalize learning for all teachers. This collaborative approach encourages districts to share their most valuable resource—human capital—through leveraging the collective talents of their staffs. As districts develop a more global view to professional learning, teachers have a larger network available at their fingertips, which can and now should include cross-district collaboration. Once teachers develop the twenty-first century mind-set, the traditional roadblocks of time and location become obsolete and, thus, are no longer a barrier to professional transformation.

Professional Learning Is Engaging

On a daily basis, school leaders challenge classroom teachers with creating engaging lessons differentiated for the needs of their students. The research on engagement is clear. When students are highly engaged in the content, learning soars. Common sense also indicates that the more involved we are with something, the more connected to it we will be. The same holds true for professional learning. When teachers have the opportunity to recommend and select sessions, work collaboratively with colleagues, develop professional relationships via social media, and create their own learning opportunities, their engagement skyrockets. Want a real-life example? Simply watch adults engage in something personal on their phones for hours at a time. Dynamic personalized, professional learning mirrors a dynamic, personalized classroom.

Professional Learning
Is Relevant and On-Demand

In a traditional professional learning model, teachers are often left asking, "How does this help me?" "Why are we doing this?" or "How is this worth our time?" These questions raise valid concerns regarding the use of time and the relevancy of the learning that is (or is supposed to be) occurring. The mind-set shift to the twenty-first century professional learner enables teachers to no longer ask the "why" or "how" but now answer these questions as learners and designers themselves. Professional learning becomes relevant for teachers when they are a vital part of the process, their voice matters, and they are encouraged to design and take ownership of their own learning. With the ability to take advantage of these personalized resources around the clock, on-demand professional learning not only becomes possible but the preferred method of growth for many.

Tool Spotlight: Voxer

Voxer, available for iOS and Android and on the web, is a push-to-talk, live messaging application that allows live voice to be simultaneously recorded, delivered, and stored in the cloud. Voxer also integrates text, photo, and location sharing. Groups of educators are now collaborating in real time by using this technology to discuss best practices, current trends, and instructional pedagogy. Examples include collaborating on a second-grade lesson on anacondas, discussing brain-friendly learning spaces, or even communicating with all stakeholders in an emergency situation. Limited only by a fifteen-minute recording, teachers are engaging in meaningful and relevant conversations in a highly personalized fashion using this tool. Check out the #eduvoxers hashtag on social media for more.

Tom Whitford (@twhitford), principal of Miller, Oakdale, and Camp Douglas Elementary Schools, Tomah Area School District, Tomah, Wisconsin

Whitford shares these insights on Voxer:

While I have benefitted from many technologies and web tools, perhaps the biggest game changer for me has become Voxer. Although I initiate many of my professional interactions on Twitter, Voxer has become the app I can use to have extended, deeper conversations on a variety of topics. I can create my own personalized podcast with hosts of my own choosing. It allows me to have a group of experts on call to discuss professional learning communities, another group to discuss technology integration, and yet another for leadership challenges. Voxer allows me to have discussions instead of just reading 140-character text messages. I can still share photos or links to articles or videos, but now I can also use tone, emotion, and even sarcasm, in ways that are easily understood by all parties involved. But most importantly, Voxer has allowed me to truly become friends with a host of amazing educators all around the world. Our conversations go beyond education and we connect on a personal and professional level about things we have in common, and that kind of support and trust only comes from getting to know your connections on a deeper level.

Shifting the Focus
Forward

"Teacher growth is closely related to pupil growth. Probably nothing within a school has more impact on students in terms of skills development, self-confidence, or classroom behavior than the personal and professional growth of their teachers."

—Roland Barth

The time is now to look forward, not backward, when envisioning what professional learning for teachers can and should look like. The stakes are simply too high not to act. Although we argue for a new, personalized approach to professional learning for all teachers, we do so not only because we think it is best for teachers but also because we believe passionately it is what is best for our students. We agree with Barth, who suggests in the chapter-opening quote that student growth is directly influenced by teacher growth. The more our teachers grow and learn, the more likely it is that our students will grow and learn as well.

There may be no time in the history of education witness to as many shifts as we are now experiencing. Our curricular standards have shifted, and with them new national assessments are being administered. We are moving from traditional textbooks and resources to online versions. Charter schools, home schooling, and other alternatives to traditional school campuses are on the rise. Many school districts are moving to 1:1 or Bring Your Own Device (BYOD) learning environments. Most significant, for the purposes of this book, is the shift in teacher evaluation, a shift that calls for ever-increasing accountability in education in which not only schools and school districts are held accountable for student performance but also individual teachers, whose evaluations will now be tied, in part, to their students' growth. In our experience, world class teachers do not shy away from accountability; in fact, they welcome such responsibility, knowing that the impact they make in the social, emotional, and academic lives of their students is immense. However, if we are to hold all teachers accountable for student performance, our next big shift in education must be teachers' professional learning: we must support their learning to ensure that their individual professional learning needs are met. The learning must be not only professional but personal. We cannot keep demanding more of our teachers unless we are willing to provide them with the support they need to meet these demands.

> If we are to hold all teachers accountable for student performance, our next big shift in education must be teachers' professional learning.

COMMON CORE SHIFTS REQUIRE
SHIFTS IN PROFESSIONAL LEARNING

Common Core State Standards (CCSS) have been adopted by an overwhelming number of states in our nation. Other nations around the world are also examining and revising the standards they expect all students to master in a given time. In order for students to master such standards, we need to ensure that teachers are equipped to support them. Six instructional shifts of teachers—three each for English language arts and mathematics—are required in order to truly align curricular materials and classroom instruction with the new Common Core standards (Common Core State Standards Initiative, 2014). These shifts range from the need to engage our students more regularly with more complex text and academic language in reading, to pursuing conceptual understanding, procedural skills and fluency, and application with equal intensity in mathematics.

When we shift our expectations for student learning, including the type of assignments in which we engage them and the ways in which they will demonstrate their learning, logic dictates that we must also shift our expectations for teacher learning. In the opening pages of this book, we suggested that traditional professional learning experiences for teachers tend to be top-down, one-size-fits-all, hours-based, and "sit and get." Clearly, the shifts we must make in the area of professional learning must focus on moving away from these four cornerstones of traditional professional learning experiences to a more authentic and more personalized vision, tailoring what we provide each teacher to his or her individual learning needs and goals. Although one can debate the relative merits of the CCSS interminably, we view these new standards as an opportunity to shift not only what we expect from our students but also what we must provide to our teachers in order to ensure that all students succeed in meeting the new performance expectations.

FROM "SAGE ON THE STAGE" TO "GUIDE ON THE SIDE" TO "MEDDLER IN THE MIDDLE"

By now, we suspect that every educator in the world has heard of another mind-set shift in education made popular several years ago, the shift from serving in the classroom as the "sage on the stage" to serving as the "guide on the side." However, we are now shifting yet again, suggesting that the teacher (or, in terms of adult learning, the provider of support, instruction, and resources) should be neither wholly "on stage" nor limited solely to "standing by the side" of the learners with whom they are working. Instead, the ideal metaphor to consider when determining how best to serve learners (whether student or adult) is the teacher as the "meddler in the middle."

McWilliam (2007) writes about the differences among the three teacher-role analogies, arguing that although there is a place for all three in classrooms, depending on the learning goals and learning styles of the learners, the meddler-in-the-middle analogy is the model most likely to reposition teachers as codirectors of the learning environment. In the classroom environment, the "sage" according to McWilliam, is likely to lead the learning at the front of the room, giving answers and expecting students to regurgitate these answers later. The "guide" may become concerned if students begin to show stress when they can't find a solution quickly. Guides may respond by giving lots of hints and suggestions. In doing so, they can unwittingly take the challenge out of the task. McWilliam suggests that a difficulty with the guide model is that it can become an excuse for passivity on the part of the teacher after tasks have been assigned. By taking on the "meddler" role, however, the "provider" is an active *partner* in the learning but not the primary *director* of the learning, which remains in the hands of learners themselves. The meddler does not jump in to save students from the struggle that rigorous authentic learning requires by giving them answers or templates for finding answers. Meddlers permit their students to experience the risks and confusion of authentic learning by allowing them to stay in the gray, as opposed to black and white, area of active learning, supporting all attempts by their students to experiment with possibilities in ways that put their lack of knowledge and need for new learning to work.

This analogy is as apt for teacher learning as it is for student learning. As we have stated throughout this book, professional learning for teachers should be highly personalized, meaning it is based on the following:

- The unique interests, individual styles, and specific needs of individual teachers
- Asking each teacher, "What is best for you?"
- Understanding each teacher's zone of proximal development and providing the teacher the opportunity to access resources to progress at his or her personal rate
- Meeting teachers where they are, determining where they need to be, and supporting them to close this gap
- Allowing teachers to learn at their own pace, using the tools that help them learn
- Aligning what we need our students to know and be able to do with what our teachers need to know and be able to do

District and school administrators need not serve merely as passive spectators in our vision of personalized learning plans (PLPs) for teachers. Instead, they are active meddlers in the middle, moving back and forth between discovering what each teacher needs to grow and learn, and what grade-level and content area teams of teachers need to grow and learn, and then providing that support, knowing it can look different in terms of content, delivery, and setting for different teachers and teaching teams. They work creatively to make, not find, the necessary time for teachers to observe other teachers, for teachers to plan and learn together, and for teachers to visit other schools or attend professional learning events when such learning opportunities are part of the personalized plan for learning. At times, administrators do stand in front of a group of teachers and share their own learning. At other times, they sit at the side of a teacher, learning alongside with the teacher. Still more often, they are in the middle connecting the teacher with the resource needed to meet that teacher's learning goals. They monitor the PLPs, reviewing these with individual teachers—and teams of job-alike teachers, when appropriate; collaboratively reflecting on the learning; and determining whether goals were met, including the next steps in the plan and how best to accomplish them. Although the learning is teacher focused, it requires the active support, encouragement, monitoring, and—in the most positive and collaborative sense of the word—meddling on the part of school and district leaders.

A CALL TO ACTION

As educators, our core business is learning. We fulfill a multitude of additional important roles, yet, at its essence, education is about learning, and our schools and school districts must be learning-focused organizations. Of course, when we talk about learning as our core business, we (rightly) think, first and foremost, of student learning. Our very finest educators share a passion for ensuring that every student they serve learns and grows to his or her absolute ultimate potential, with the standards they are charged with teaching serving as the *floor* of student learning for all students but the *ceiling* for none. Since our core business remains student growth and learning, it certainly stands to reason that teacher growth and learning is nearly, if not equally, as important. Teachers who model lifelong learning, continuously expanding their knowledge base and skillset, are much more likely to produce students who follow suit. We do not believe that the traditional model for teacher learning has enjoyed widespread success, and it now merits serious consideration for schools worldwide. The time has come for a new vision for professional learning.

This new vision for transforming teachers' learning begins with the name itself, which focuses on "learning." As humans, we are instinctually curious beings and intrinsically motivated to learn. As educational leaders, we must seize on this natural phenomenon and extend, rather than mute, this natural inclination to pursue new knowledge and skills. In addition to emphasizing professional learning, or growth, as opposed to development, we also feel strongly about emphasizing the "personal," not just "professional," component of personalized learning plans for teachers. Such plans are not only *professional*, they are *personal*, meaning they are designed based on the unique strengths, needs, interests, and job responsibilities of the individual teacher. They include the six components outlined in Chapter 3:

- Teacher voice is at the heart of the plan's roadmap.
- Seat time is irrelevant. The learning outcome is what matters most.
- Professional learning occurs in both formal and informal environments.
- Nontraditional forms of professional learning (e.g., blogging, social media, Twitter chats, Edcamps) are recognized as valuable learning experiences.
- Teachers are responsible for learning outcomes and must be able to communicate how their learning has improved their craft; specifically, how their personal growth has improved classroom experiences for students.
- A supervisor's input is a vital part of the plan, yielding a collaboratively designed roadmap for professional growth.

(For an example of a personalized learning plan for teachers, please visit the Connected Educators companion website.)

Effective professional learning mirrors effective classroom instruction. It is structured yet flexible. It is teacher-focused yet a collaborative venture between each teacher and a building leader or leaders. It allows for a great deal of teacher choice and teacher voice within a system of professional learning expectations and mind-sets. It is based on the needs of individual teachers and provides real-world, practical learning experiences that allow teachers to become better at what they do. Effective professional learning—like effective classroom teaching—results in more actively engaged participants and, ultimately, improved results. Students do not want their time wasted on busywork assignments and impersonal learning activities. Not surprisingly, neither do teachers. The time we have available to focus on professional learning—no matter how creative we are—is not nearly enough, so we do not have a minute to waste. We live in a world in which learning—including teacher learning—can occur anytime and anywhere. School leaders must take advantage of this opportunity and allow teachers more freedom in how they pursue their own learning.

In the classroom, personalized learning—also called "competency-based learning"—allows students to master skills at their own pace with innovative technologies and support systems. We call on school districts around the world to establish similar systems for teacher learning. We realize that such a model takes more time and effort than traditional systems. We also realize this can be a messy, nonlinear model for professional learning. Ultimately, however, the results we achieve make it worthwhile, as this new model is focused on teachers' strengths and addressing their challenges in a way that empowers them to take control of their learning and become better at what they do. It results in teachers who are more engaged in their own learning and, in turn, more engaged in the learning of their students. As educators ourselves, part of our personal and professional mission—regardless of the various roles in which we have served—has been to work in a way that will make our students' tomorrow better than today. Transforming professional learning for our children's teachers is a matter of urgency and a primary way we can fulfill this mission. Our kids—and their teachers—are worth and deserve the effort!

References

Common Core State Standards Initiative. (2014). *Other resources*. Retrieved August 2, 2014, from http://www.corestandards.org.

DuFour, R., DuFour, R., Eaker, R., & Many, T. (2006). *Learning by doing: A handbook for professional learning communities at work*. Bloomington, IN: Solution Tree.

Dweck, C. (2007). *Mindset: The new psychology of success*. New York, NY: Ballantine Books.

Fullan, M. (2014). *The principal: Three keys to maximizing impact*. San Francisco, CA: Jossey-Bass.

Guskey, T. R., & Yoon, K. S. (2009). What works in professional development. *Phi Delta Kappan, 90*, 495–50s0. doi:10.1177/003172170909000709

McWilliam, E. (2007, January 8–10). *Unlearning how to teach*. Presented at Higher Education Academy at University of Wales Institute, Cardiff, Australia. Retrieved from http://creativityconference07.org/presented_papers/McWilliam_Unlearning.doc.

Professional Learning Community. (2014). Retrieved July 27, 2014, from *The glossary of education reform*, https://edglossary.org/professional-learning-community.

Vygotsky, L. (1962). *Thought and language* (E. Hanfmann & G. Vakar, Trans. & Eds.). Cambridge, MA: MIT Press.

Whitaker, T. (2003). *What great teachers do differently: 14 things that matter most*. New York, NY: Routledge.

A SAGE Company

Corwin is committed to improving education for all learners by publishing books and other professional development resources for those serving the field of PreK–12 education. By providing practical, hands-on materials, Corwin continues to carry out the promise of its motto: **"Helping Educators Do Their Work Better."**